Salem Witch Trials

The True Story Behind The Infamous Witch Trials of 1692

Anna Revell

Copyright © 2017.

All rights reserved. No part of this publication may be reproduced, distributed, or transmitted in any form or by any means, including photocopying, recording, or other electronic or mechanical methods, without the prior written permission of the publisher, except in the case of brief quotations embodied in critical reviews and certain other noncommercial uses permitted by copyright law.

This book is intended for informational and entertainment purposes only. The publisher limits all liability arising from this work to the fullest extent of the law.

Table of Contents

Introduction

The Initial Accusation

Further Accusations Are Made

The Court of Oyer and Terminer

The Workings of a Witch Trial

How The Salem Witch Trials Are Concluded and Their Aftermath

Introduction

The belief in the supernatural, and its ability to harm an individual had emerged in Europe in the 14th century. This sparked a series of witch trials across the continent.

By the mid 17th century this trend was gradually dying out across much of Europe. However, accusations of witchcraft, and the hysteria which accompanies such a case, would sporadically occur in some places such as the American Colonies up until the early 18th century. The most prominent example of this was the Salem Witch Trials, these occurred in Salem, New England between 1692 and 1693.

The state of New England had been settled by religious refugees who, after being persecuted in England, traveled to the new world where they sought a new life in a new land. These religious refugees were known as Puritans.

The Puritans were influenced in part by Calvinism. They opposed many of the traditions of the Anglican Church of England. These included the use of the Book of Common Prayer, the wearing of priestly vestments during services, kneeling during the sacrament and the use of the Holy Cross during baptismal services. These things were considered by the Puritans to be popery.

The head of the Church of England, King Charles I, was hostile to the Puritans point of view, this led to Anglican Church officials embarking on a campaign designed to repress these dissenting views.

By the end of the 1630s, some Puritans had fled England for refuge in more sympathetic countries such as the Netherlands. The vast majority opted to head to North America.

Once in North America, the Puritans hoped to establish a strict, bible based society. Here they would be free to worship and conduct themselves in the manner they believed was correct.

While initially many Puritans made the journey the Civil War in England and subsequent victory by Cromwell's Puritan-dominated Parliamentarian forces, slowed the flow of migration.

The eventual failure of the republic led to the restoration of the monarchy in England and, consequently, the continued exodus of Puritans. Meanwhile, in North America, the earlier settlers had established thriving communities.

In some places, such as Massachusetts a successful merchant class emerged. In these places, the communities were significantly less religiously motivated than in other settlements.

For those who remained steadfast to their puritanical beliefs life in the new world was not always easy. Tensions existed between the puritanical colonies and other settlers who lacked the same adherence to their religion. There were also tensions between the settlers and the natives.

In New England Native Americans, who were attempting to regain land that had originally belonged to them, attacked many settlements. This led to some settlements being abandoned and a flood of refugees into areas such as Essex County.

In some strict puritanical settlements, the entrance of these refugees, who were not always of the same religious conviction, created tensions in the once harmonious communities.

The area in which the Salem Witch Trials occurred centered around the, now, city of Salem, Massachusetts. As well as Salem accusations and trials took place in the neighboring Salem Village as well as in the nearby towns of Ipswich and Andover.

Salem Village, today known as Danvers, was well known for its fractious population. It had numerous disputes with the neighboring town of Salem. These arguments frequently centered on issues such as property lines and grazing rights.

Another frequent topic of dispute was church privileges. In 1672 the village of Salem had voted to hire a minister of their own- separate from the town of Salem. The first two ministers hired by the village, James Bayley and George Burroughs departed not long into their tenures.

James Bayley stayed from 1673 until 1679, while George Burroughs lasted barely three years, 1680 to 1683. The main reason for their departures was that the villagers had failed to pay their full rate.

A third minister, Deodat Lawson, also stayed for only a brief period. Lawson chose to leave as the church in Salem had refused to ordain him. The wider parish disagreed with the Salem Village's choice for its next, and first ordained, minister.

On the 18th of June 1689, the church of Salem Village agreed to hire Samuel Parris as minister. He was to be paid sixty-six pounds a year. One-third of this sum would be paid in money while the other two thirds would be in the form of provisions. Parris was also granted the use of the parsonage.

In October 1869 Parris was granted the deeds to the parsonage and two acres of land. This conflicted with an 1861 resolution the village had passed which stated that "it shall not be lawful for the inhabitants of this village to convey the houses or lands or any other concerns belonging to the Ministry to any particular persons or person: not for any cause by vote or other ways".

While on the surface this may seem like a gesture of thanks from a village grateful for his wise ministry, in reality, Parris was not an ideal fit for the village. Numerous accounts show that he was constantly unable to settle the disputes of his fractious parishioners.

Parris often sought out "iniquitous" behavior in his congregation and would make well-regarded church members suffer public penance for minor misdemeanors. In short, Parris significantly stoked the tensions within the village of Salem.

In the years leading up to 1692 rumors had spread of witchcraft being practiced in the towns and villages around Salem. Cotton Mather, who was a minister of Boston's North Church, published numerous pamphlets some of which showcased his belief in witchcraft.

In one book, 'Memorable Providences Relating to Witchcrafts and Possessions' (1689), Mather described his observations on the subject. He also detailed how witchcraft had affected the children of John Goodwin a Boston mason. Mather told how the eldest Goodwin child had been tempted by the devil to steal linen from a washerwoman named Goody Glover.

In return Glover, who was described by her husband as a witch, cast spells on the Goodwin's children. Subsequently, four of the six children began to suffer from strange fits. These fits were accompanied by other symptoms such as neck and back pains, loud and random outbursts or screaming fits and a seeming loss of control of their bodies. It wasn't long before witchcraft had been ascribed as the cause of these symptoms.

Blame soon fell on Goody Glover. In the staunchly puritanical society, Glover was already something of an oddity, a Roman Catholic, Irish peasant. As a result, she was an easy target for the superstitious mob.

 After being arrested Glover supposedly confessed to praying to many spirits. While her accusers saw this as a confession that Glover spoke to the devil and her minions Glover could have just as easily been referring to the Catholic saints.

Following her trial, Goody Glover became the last person to be hung in Boston for witchcraft. The symptoms displayed by the Goodwin children would help to fuel the craze and subsequent witch trials that would grip Salem and the surrounding area in 1692.

The Initial Accusation

In February 1692 Betty Parris, the nine-year-old daughter of the Reverend Samuel Parris and her cousin, eleven-year-old Abigail Williams began to suffer from fits.

These fits were described as being "beyond the power of epileptic fits or natural disease". In addition to the fits, the two girls would scream, hurl objects across the room and make strange, inhuman sounds.

The pair would also reportedly crawl under furniture and were often found contorted into peculiar positions. As well as members of their family these episodes were witnessed by many people including John Hale, the minister of the nearby town of

Beverly, and Reverend Deodat Lawson, the former minister of the village of Salem.

When examined the girls told physicians that they often felt as if they were being pinched or pricked with pins. After examining both girls one doctor assumed to be William Griggs, concluded that there was no physical evidence of any ailment.

Soon other girls and young women in the village were exhibiting similar symptoms. When Deodat Lawson returned to preach as a guest in the Salem Village meetinghouse his sermon was interrupted several times by outbursts from women suffering fits.

Among those suffering from the mysterious disease included Betty Parris, Abigail Williams, Ann Putnam Jr (who was only twelve years old) and Elizabeth Hubbard.

With no physical cause to be found the suspicion soon fell on witchcraft.

With rumors and whispered accusations spreading throughout Salem Village the finger of blame had fallen on three women; Sarah Good, Sarah Osborne, and Tituba.

The first of the three women, Sarah Good, had been born in Wenham, Massachusetts Bay Colony in 1653 to John and Elizabeth Solar. Despite John Solart being a prosperous man when he died Sarah and her sisters were left without an inheritance. Her first marriage to Daniel Poole, a laborer, had ended with his death in 1682.

Poole's death left Sarah deep in debt. This debt became the responsibility of William Good upon his marriage to Sarah. As the Goods could not handle the debt they were reduced to begging. By 1692 the couple were homeless. It was in this condition that the Goods arrived in Salem Village.

As far as the people of Salem were concerned Sarah Good was a filthy, bad-tempered woman who was detached from the rest of the village. She was often associated with the death of the villager's livestock.

At her, later trial witnesses told how Sarah Good would knock on their door asking for charity. If her request was refused she would walk away muttering, what the villagers assumed were, curses.

In her defense Sarah Good claimed that she was reciting the Ten Commandments. However when asked to, at her trial, Sarah Good was unable to recite a single one.

The second woman to be accused was Sarah Osborne. Married to a prominent New England man named Robert Prince, the couple moved to Salem Village in 1662. Here they raised two sons named Joseph and James and a daughter named Elizabeth. Her husband's death in 1674 left Sarah widowed.

Osborne was considered an outcast in the village due to her non-attendance at church. In truth her three-year absence from worship was down to a long illness as well as legal issues within her extended family; Robert Princes' brother had married into the powerful Putnam family. It has since been suggested that the accusations against Osborne were the result of influence from the Putnam family.

That Osborne had, after her first husband's death, married an indentured servant added to the feelings of mistrust the villagers of Salem held towards her. Many also disapproved of what they perceived as Sarah Osborne's attempts to control her son's inheritance.

The third woman to be accused was Tituba. An enslaved woman who was owned by Samuel Parris, it is believed that Tituba arrived in the United States via Barbados from either South or Central America. It is thought that Parris acquired Tituba while in Barbados.

Tituba was married to John Indian another servant to the Parris family. A Native American, who was possibly from Central America, John Indian would later become one of the accusers in the Salem Witch Trials, testifying against his wife.

Tituba was the first person to be accused by the two girls and despite initially denying her involvement later confessed to being involved in witchcraft. This confession came after a beating by Samuel Parris.

Tituba claimed that she had made a "witch cake" in an attempt to find the identity of the itch ho had cursed the girls. She also confessed to having knowledge of white magic and occult techniques. Her previous mistress in Barbados had taught these things to Tituba so that the slave would be able to defend herself.

Tituba would accuse many other men and women from Salem Village and the surrounding villages of being witches. She also talked about black dogs, hogs, colored birds, rats, cats, foxes, and wolves. Tituba accused Sarah Osborne of possessing a creature with the head of a woman, two legs, and wings.

The record of Tituba's pre-trial examination holds her giving an energetic confession. During this Tituba spoke before the court of "creatures who inhabit the invisible world," and "the dark rituals which bind them together in service of Satan".

Tituba also implicated both Good and Osborne while asserting, "many other people in the colony were engaged in the devil's conspiracy against the Bay." Tituba's confessions confused those who heard it. It also led to many of the villagers believing that Satan was walking the streets of Salem.

As is often the case in witch trials the three women accused were all considered outcasts in one way or another. After an appearance in front of the local magistrates, the three accused were interrogated for several days. On the first of March 1692 Sarah Good, Sarah Osborne, and Tituba were imprisoned.

While Sarah Good was executed for her crimes and Sarah Osborne would die in prison Tituba was eventually exonerated.

Further Accusations Are Made

The imprisonment of the three women did not stop accusations of witchcraft. Over the course of March further people were also accused.

Martha Corey, a pious and God-fearing woman who was unaware of the rising levels of paranoia in the village, expressed skepticism about the credibility of the girl's accusations. Upon hearing this two other girls, Ann Putman Jr and Mercy Lewis accused Corey of witchcraft.

Like Corey, Rebecca Nurse was known in Salem Village to be a regular worshipper and a pious, God fearing woman. The accusations against Nurse and Corey troubled the community greatly as they were both upstanding, pious pillars of the community. If they could be witches then, so the townspeople thought, nobody was safe from Satan's temptations. At 71, Rebecca Nurse was also one of the oldest accused.

Next to find the finger of accusation pointing at them was four years old Dorothy Good, the daughter of Sarah Good. Mary Walcott and Ann Putnam Jr claimed that the child was out of control and, despite her young age, had been seen cavorting with her mother and the devil. The magistrates questioned Dorothy and her unwitting answers were interpreted as a confession that implicated her mother.

The fourth person to be accused during March was Rachel Clinton. Not a resident of

Salem but the nearby town of Ipswich, Rachel Clinton had been forced to become a beggar after the breakdown of her marriage to Lawrence Clinton. Like Sarah Good, Clinton was an outcast of society. She was, therefore, an easy target.

Rachel Clinton was arrested on charges of witchcraft at the end of March. These charges were unrelated to the afflicted girls in the village of Salem. Rachel Clinton died destitute at the end of 1694.

Next to be accused were Sarah Cloyce, the sister of Rebecca Nurse and Elizabeth (Bassett) Proctor. Sarah Cloyce had found herself the victim of suspicion after defending her sister. Sarah had pointedly walked out of church, slamming the door shut behind her when Rebecca was denounced. Soon after this Sarah Cloyce found herself accused of afflicting Mary Walcott and Abigail Williams.

Despite being an upstanding member of the community Elizabeth Proctor was descended from Quakers. The Puritan community held Quakers and their beliefs in great suspicion.

In addition, Elizabeth's grandmother was known for her cures and medicinal potions. This was enough for the accusations by Abigail Williams, Mary Warren (a servant in the Proctor house) and Mercy Lewis to be taken seriously.

The accused appeared before the local magistrates John Hathorne and Jonathan Corwin, who were also members of the influential Governor's Council, in April of 1692. Also present for the women's examinations were Deputy Governor Thomas Danforth and assistants Samuel Sewall, Samuel Appleton, James Russell and Isaac Addington.

Both women proclaimed their innocence. The husband of Elizabeth Proctor, John Proctor was arrested during the proceedings for constantly objecting and proclaiming his wife's innocence.

Within a week Giles Corey, the husband of Martha Corey and a covenanted church member in the town of Salem had been arrested, accused of being a warlock. Also arrested were Abigail Hobbs and her stepmother Deliverance Hobbs, Bridget Bishop and Mary Warren. The later had previously accused Elizabeth Proctor of the same charges she was now accused of.

Under rigorous examination, Abigail Hobbs, Deliverance Hobbs, and Mary Warren soon confessed to the crimes. The three went on to name a number of additional people as accomplices.

These accusations led to even more arrests. William Hobbs, the husband of Deliverance Hobbs and the father of Sarah was accused, as were Nehemiah Abbott Jr, Mary English, Edward Bishop Jr, and his wife Sarah Bishop.

Also arrested was Sarah Wildes. Her husband's first wife had been a cousin to the Putnam family, one of the primary accusers in the Salem Witch Trials. It is thought that a family feud was the basis for the accusations against Wildes, as had been the case with the accusations against Sarah Osborne.

The final person to be arrested during this spell was Mary Eastey. Mary was the sister of Rebecca Nurse and Sarah Cloyce, like her sisters she had been a pious and respected member of the community. Mercy Lewis, a servant of the Putnam family, accused Eastey of witchcraft.

Mercy Lewis claimed to be suffering from fits, which continued until Eastey was arrested. Mary Eastey was later accused, along with her sister Sarah Cloyce, of possessing both their late brother and their niece.

During the course of April, Nehemiah Abbott Jr was released after his accusers agreed that he was not the person afflicting them. Mary Eastey was also released for a similar reason before being quickly rearrested on the same charges.

On the 30th of April, Philip English the husband of Mary English was arrested along with Sarah Morey Lydia Dustin, Dorcas Hoar and Susannah Martin.

Also arrested was the reverend George Burroughs. Born in Suffolk, England Burroughs had been raised and educated in America, graduating from Harvard College with honors in 1670. Ten years later in 1680 Burroughs was appointed minister in Salem Village where he served for three years before moving to other parishes in Maine.

It is thought that people were disgruntled over the manner in which Burroughs had left his Salem Village parish. Some disgruntled parishioners took the opportunity provided by the witch trials to accuse their former minister in an attempt to gain some form of retribution. Because of these accusations, Burroughs was the only minister to be executed during the Salem Witch Trials.

Throughout the course of May accusations of witchcraft and illicit pacts with the devil continued to be made. Some of those suspected managed to evade capture, presumably forewarned by those sympathetic to their plight. Multiple warrants were issued before John Willard and Elizabeth Colson were finally arrested while George Jacobs Jr and Daniel Andrews managed to escape completely.

Warrants were issued for a further thirty-six people while examinations and interrogations continued apace in Salem

Village. Sarah Dustin, the daughter of Lydia Dustin, along with Ann Sears, Bethiah Carter Sr and her daughter Bethiah Carter Jr, John Willard, Alice Parker, Ann Pudeator, Abigail Soames, Daniel Andrew, Sarah Buckley and her daughter Mary Witheridge were questioned. Some of these were detained while others are released.

Also under suspicion were many members of the Jacobs family. While George Jr managed to evade arrest his father George Sr was not so lucky. George Sr's daughter in law Rebecca Jacobs and granddaughter Margaret Jacobs gave evidence against him and eventually George Sr was convicted.

Also falling into the now wide-ranging net of suspicion was Elizabeth Colson, Elizabeth Hart, Thomas Farrar Sr, Roger Toothaker and his wife Mary Toothaker and their daughter Margaret.

The daughter of Elizabeth and John Proctor, Sarah Proctor, and her brother William Proctor along with Elizabeth Proctor's sisters in law Sarah Bassett and Mary DeRich were also accused. As were Susannah Roots, Sarah Pease, Elizabeth Cary, Martha Carrier, Elizabeth Fosdick, Wilmot Redd, Sarah Rice, Elizabeth Howe, Captain John Alden and Arthur Abbott.

On the 27th of May 1692, William Phips ordered the establishment of a Special Court of Oyer and Terminer to prosecute those in jail. By the time the court convened sixty-two people had been arrested.

The Court of Oyer and Terminer

Translated from old Anglo-French Oyer and Terminer translates as "to hear and determine". In Law French, this was one of the names for the commission by which a judge of assize sat.

Up until 1972 in England and Wales assizes were courts that sat quarterly throughout the year and heard the more serious cases; minor offenses being dealt with by justices of the peace in petty sessions or magistrates courts.

The court of Oyer and Terminer was sometimes referred to by other names; either the Law Latin name audiendo et terminado or the Old English name soc and sac.

Once called the court of Oyer and Terminer would make diligent inquiries into the crimes committed. Often these inquiries were made on behalf of the sitting judges. The case would them be called and heard before the court.

When all the evidence for both the prosecution and defense had been presented the petit jury or trial jury would deliberate before announcing their verdict. The judges would then pass sentence.

The petit jury or trial jury comprises of between six to twelve people. The petit jury will hear a case before deliberating the evidence and coming to a conclusion of guilty or not guilty.

It differs from a grand jury in that a grand jury does not pass verdict on the guilt or innocence but merely deliberates whether there is enough evidence for a case to be heard before the court. The grand jury also has more members, anywhere from fifteen to twenty-three people can sit on a grand jury.

The governor of Massachusetts, William Phipps, created a court of Oyer and Terminer to oversee the Salem Witch Trials. The court consisted of A Mr. Stoughton, Major Richard, Major Gindy, Mr. Wait Winthrop, Captain Sam Sewall, Mr. Sargeant and Major Nathaniel Saltonstall.

At the court's first sitting William Stoughton, the Lieutenant General took on the role of Chief Magistrate. Thomas Newton was acting as the Crown's Attorney presenting the prosecuting cases while Stephen Sewall took on the role of clerk of the court.

The first case brought before the grand jury was that of Bridget Bishop. She was described before the court as not living a Puritan lifestyle. In such a rigid society her style of dressed marked her out; Bishop wore black clothing and "odd" costumes which were against the Puritan code. This along with her supposedly immoral lifestyle marked her out as a witch.

After hearing the evidence the grand jury endorsed all the indictments against Bridget Bishop. Events now moved quickly. Her case was heard later on the same day and she was quickly found guilty. Convicted of witchcraft Bridget Bishop was executed by hanging on the 10th of June 1692.

The day after Bishop's indictment hearing and trial the grand jury heard and endorsed indictments against Rebecca Nurse and John Willard. Unlike Bishop's case, these two cases did not go immediately to trial.

Immediately following Bridget Bishop's execution the court of Oyer and Terminer adjourned until the 30th of June. During this break, the court intended to seek advice from New England's most influential ministers upon the state of things in Salem.

The collective response of the ministers came back on the 15th of June, composed by Cotton Mather. In it, the ministers expressed concern for those suffering "molestations from the invisible world" and called for help from all persons. The ministers also thank God for helping to detect "the abominable witchcrafts" in the community.

The response was not a ringing endorsement for the witch trails, however. The ministers also advised caution, warning that not too much weight should be placed on "things received only upon the Devil's authority" for he may work to get "an advantage over us".

Despite these words of caution, the ministers did not go as far as to call for the dismissal of all spectral and circumstantial evidence. Instead, they pressed the need for the case to be resolved quickly.

It is thought that the reluctance by the ministers to ban spectral evidence was the underlying motive behind Major Nathaniel Saltonstall's resignation from his post on the court of Oyer and Terminer. Mr. J Corwin replaced him. Corwin had been one of the two main judges who had heard the early cases in Salem Village.

The effect of the letter by the ministers was to see prosecutions continue with more vigor than before and it seems that while those in Salem took the advice that the case should be resolved quickly and thoroughly all words advising caution were ignored.

As the court of Oyer and Terminer prepared to sit again more people were arrested and examined. By now the cases had spread from the Salem Village to the town of Salem. Meanwhile, John Hathorne and Bartholomew Gedney had joined Jonathan Corwin in the court of Oyer and Terminer, both were local magistrates.

On the 16th of June Roger Toothaker died in prison still a suspect.

From the end of June until early July the grand juries under the guidance of the court of Oyer and Terminer endorsed indictments against Sarah Good, Elizabeth Howe, Susannah Martin, Elizabeth Proctor, John Proctor, Martha Carrier, Sarah Wildes and Dorcas Hoar.

From these the cases of Good, Howe, Martin, Wildes along with the case against Rebecca Nurse went to trial almost immediately. All five were found guilty. The women were executed by hanging on the 19th of July 1692.

During July Ann Foster, her daughter Mary Lacey Sr., and granddaughter Mary Lacey Jr. all confessed to the charge of being witches. Meanwhile, Anthony Checkley was appointed by Governor Phips to replace Thomas Newton as the Crown's Attorney.

Newton had decided to leave proceedings to take up a position in New Hampshire.

In August the grand jury indicted a further four people; George Burroughs, Mary Eastey, Martha Corey and George Jacobs Sr. At their trials Martha Carries, George Jacobs Sr, George Burroughs, John Willand and Elizabeth and John Proctor were convicted of the charges against them.

On the 19th of August, the group was executed with the exception of Elizabeth Proctor. She had been granted a temporary stay of execution after it was discovered that she was pregnant.

The condemned were transported from the prison on a cart through the streets of Salem Village. Crowds of people turned up to watch their final journey and execution.

At the gallows site, as George Burroughs was being prepared he made a speech proclaiming his innocence. He followed this by reciting the Lords Prayer- people believed that witches were unable to recite the Lord's Prayer.

Burroughs' oration was so well composed and delivered with such a fervency of spirit that many in the crowd were affected. Some were moved to tears. It also served to turn the opinion of many in the crowd, the general consensus was now of the opinion that Burroughs was innocent.

Sensing the change in mood the authorities started to worry that the crowd would try to stop the execution. Burroughs was quickly hanged.

After Burroughs had died Cotton Mather addressed the crowd and told them that Burroughs had been transformed into "the Angel of Light". This served to appease the crowd and the executions continued unhindered.

During September the grand jury indicted a further eighteen people. William Proctor, however, was not indicted by the grand jury and his case was dismissed. He was quickly re-arrested in new charges.

On the 19th of September, things took an even grislier turn. Giles Corey an 81-year-old farmer from an area of Salem known as Salem Farms refused to plead guilty or not guilty at an arraignment. The court ordered that Corey undergo a form of torture known as peine forte et dure.

Translated as "hard and forceful punishment" this torture saw the subject tied down before having an increasingly heavy load, often stones or rocks, placed on their chest. This punishment was often used in an attempt to draw out a plea from the subject.

In the case of Corey peine forte et dure was not successful. Still refusing to enter a plea Giles Corey died whilst undergoing the torture.

Undeterred the legal process continued. Eleven more people were tried and found guilty while four more entered a guilty plea. The 22nd of September saw a further eight executions.

During this period one of those convicted, Dorcas Hoar was given a temporary reprieve thanks to several ministers supporting her case. Meanwhile Mary Bradbury, despite being 77 at the time, managed to escape.

Like Elizabeth Proctor, it was discovered that Abigail Faulkner Sr was pregnant and she was granted a temporary stay of execution. According to some reports, this reprieve would later become a stay of charges.

Meanwhile, Cotton Mather had been granted access to the trail reports and accounts. He quickly compiled 'Wonders of the Invisible World', his account of the trials. A copy was given to the Governor of Massachusetts, William Phips when he returned to the area at the start of October.

Because of his prolonged absence from the area, Phips had not been fully aware of the situation in Salem. Now fully informed of events in the area Governor Phips took action and halted the witch trials.

In a letter sent to London, along with a copy of Mather's account of the trials, Phips wrote that he now "understood what danger some of their innocent subjects might be exposed to, if the evidence of the afflicted persons only did prevail either to the committing or trying any of them, I did before any application was made unto me about it put a stop to the proceedings of the Court and they are now stopped till their Majesties pleasure be known."

On the 29th of October, the court of Oyer and Terminer was formally dismissed on the orders of Governor Phips. It may only be a coincidence but Governor Phip's intervention coincided with his wife, Lady

Mary Phips, being one of a group recently "called out upon".

Whatever the motivation behind it the intervention of Governor Phips marked the end of executions in the Salem Witch Trials.

In January 1693 the new Superior Court of Judicature, Court of Assize and General Goal Delivery convened in Salem. William Stoughton as Chief Justice again headed it.

As with the previous court of Oyer and Terminer Anthony Checkley continued as the Attorney General with Jonathon Elatson as Clerk of the Court. It was hoped that this court, unlike previous settings, would now act in a more considered manner and would be less susceptible to being carried away in the witchcraft hysteria.

The first five cases tried were those of people who had been indicted but not tried by the court of Oyer and Terminer in the previous September. These were the cases against Sarah Buckley, Margaret Jacobs, Rebecca Jacobs, Mary Whittredge (or Witheridge) and Job Tookey. All five were found not guilty of the charges.

Meanwhile, grand jury sittings were held for the majority of those who were still in jail. While many saw their charges completely dismissed, sixteen of the prisoners were indicted and tried. Of these sixteen only three were found guilty. These were Elizabeth Johnson Jr., Sarah Wardwell, and Mary Post.

The Chief Justice William Stoughton issued the warrants for the execution of Johnson,

Wardwell, and Post along with others who had been condemned to death by the earlier court. Governor Phips promptly pardoned all these cases. Their lives had been spared.

At the end of January into early February the Superior Court of Judicature, Court of Assize and General Goal Delivery sat again, this time in Charlestown, Middlesex County. Here grand jury sessions were held and five people were tried.

All five, Sarah Cole from Lynn, Lydia and Sarah Dustin, Mary Taylor and Mary Toothaker were found not guilty however they were not released immediately. Instead, the women were held in jail until they paid their jail fees. Lydia Dustin died in jail on the 10th of March 1693.

The Superior Court of Judicature, Court of Assize and General Goal Delivery convened again at the end of April in Boston, Suffolk County. Here Captain John Alden was cleared of all charges by proclamation. The court also head charges against Mary Watkins a servant girl who was accused of falsely accusing her mistress of witchcraft.

This was followed, in May, by another sitting of the Superior Court of Judicature, Court of Assize and General Goal Delivery in Ipswich, Essex County. Here a number of grand jury sittings were held. Of the cases heard here all but five were dismissed.

The five cases, those against Susannah Post, Eunice Frye, Mary Bridges Jr., Mary Barker and William Barker Jr., subsequently went to trial where they were all found not guilty.

These were the final cases to be heard under the umbrella of the Salem Witch Trials.

The Workings of a Witch Trial

The process for sparking a witch trial was simple enough. After someone had concluded that a death or illness had been caused by witchcraft they entered a complaint against the alleged witch with the local magistrate.

If the complaint was deemed credible the magistrates would have the accused person arrested. The accused was then brought in for a public examination; this was in effect a rigorous interrogation, during which they were continually pressed to confess.

If, after this process, the magistrates were satisfied that the complaint was valid the prisoner would be handed over to a superior court. Here the grand jury would hear the case along with the evidence of any witnesses.

A person could also be indicted on charges of afflicting with witchcraft or for making an unlawful covenant with the Devil. As in the case of Bridget Bishop once indicted, the defendant went to trial that would often take place on the same day. The whole process was often swift and clinical if not fair and just.

An alleged witch or warlock would also be excommunicated from their church, often as soon as the allegations were made. As a result, they were denied proper burials. After being hung, usually in a convenient tree, their lifeless bodies were cut down and dumped into a shallow grave.

This was the grim process played out time and again in Salem.

After the crowd had dispersed and darkness had fallen oral history tells us that the families of the dead would reclaim their relatives bodies. The deceased would be reburied in unmarked graves on the family property. As records were usually kept by the church many record books of the time did not note the deaths of those executed for witchcraft.

Spectral evidence is a form of evidence-based upon dreams and visions. During the Salem Witch Trials, it was admitted into court by the appointed chief justice, William Stoughton.

Spectral evidence held that the supposed witch's spirit or specter would appear to the witness in a dream or vision, often the witch's specter would take on the form of an animal, usually a black cat or a wolf. The witness, and often accuser, would then testify that the witch via its specter had proceeded to attack or attempt to kill them in their dream.

The admittance of spectral evidence meant that the accused was held responsible for the assault even though they were elsewhere at the time.

Cotton Mather, the prominent minister, argued during the Salem Witch Trials that it was appropriate to admit spectral evidence to legal proceedings. However, Mather cautioned that any conviction should be based on more than purely spectral evidence.

He argued that it was possible for the Devil to take the shape of an innocent person.

After the Salem Witch Trials, Cotton Mather became an opponent of spectral evidence. His newfound opposition was not on the basis that spectral evidence was false testimony by witnesses, but that it might be a deception by demons.

Mather outlined this belief in 'Cases of Conscience Concerning Evil Spirits Personating Men, Witchcrafts, infallible Proofs of Guilt in such as are accused with that Crime'. Here he argued that "It were better that ten suspected witches should escape than that one innocent person should be condemned".

Meanwhile, people were beginning to speak out against the use of spectral evidence by the court. Reverend William Milbourne, a Baptist minister in Boston, publicly petitioned the General Assembly in early June 1692. Subsequently, Milbourne had to post £200 bond or face being arrested for "contriving, writing and publishing the said scandalous Papers".

This was followed by more support; twelve local ministers submitted 'The Return of several Ministers to the Governor and Council in Boston'. This text cautioned the authorities not to rely entirely on the use of spectral evidence.

Spectral evidence was not a unique feature of the Salem Witch Trials. During the same period, spectral evidence was also used in a trial in colonial Rhode Island. This saw Thomas Cornell, Jr. being convicted of matricide. The case is now believed to be an accidental death.

The use of spectral evidence in a court of law was later outlawed in the United States of America and the vast majority of countries around the world.

Another supposed form of evidence used by some during the Salem Witch Trials was that of a witch cake.

Early in February 1692 soon after Betty Parris and Abigail Williams began to suffer their fits but before specific accusations were made Mary Sibley a neighbor of Reverend Parris instructed one of his servants John Indian, to make a witch cake. Sibely intended to use traditional English white magic to discover the identity of the witch who was afflicting the girls.

The cake was made from rye meal and urine from the afflicted girls. Invisible particles the witch had sent to afflict the girls were, it was thought, in the girl's urine. The cake was then fed to a dog.

According to English folklore traditions when the dog ate the cake the witch herself would be hurt. A woman heard crying in pain as the dog ate the cake would be identified as the witch.

This strange superstition was based on the Cartesian "Doctrine of Effluvia". This held that witches afflicted others by the use of "venomous and malignant particles, that were ejected from the eye".

According to the records of the Salem Village Church, Parris spoke with Sibley in private on the 25th of March. In the conversation, she confessed to using white magic and admitted that it was a "grand error". Parris accepted Sibley's sorrowful confession and apology.

The following Sunday, during his sermon, Parris addressed his congregation on the subject of the "calamities" that were occurring in his own household. He also stated, "it never brake forth to any considerable light, until diabolical means were used, by the making of a cake by my Indian man, who had his direction from this our sister, Mary Sibly."

Parris went on to admonish and warn the entire congregation against the use of any kind of magic.

Even white magic, Parris advised, was to be avoided as it was essentially, "going to the

Devil for help against the Devil." Mary Sibley then publicly acknowledged the "error" of her actions before the congregation. After hearing this, the congregation voted by a show of hands that they were satisfied with her admission. No further action was taken against Sibley.

Despite Parris' sermon, it seems that the community continued to believe in the legitimacy of witch cakes and other forms of white magic. Instances appear in the records of one such episode demonstrate this continued belief.

Two statements made against Elizabeth Howe were comprised of accounts of people suggesting that an ear be cut off and burned from two different animals that Howe was thought to have afflicted, to prove she was the one who had bewitched them to death.

Traditionally it had been alleged that Betty Parris and Abigail Williams were often looked after and entertained by the Parris' slave Tituba. Popular rumors have claimed that she supposedly taught the two girls about voodoo in the parsonage kitchen. However, there is no contemporary evidence to support this.

A variety of secondary sources, starting with Charles W. Upham, originating in the 19th century, suggest that a circle of the girls, with Tituba's help, tried their hands at fortune telling. They used the white of an egg and a mirror to create a primitive crystal ball to divine the professions of their future spouses.

During this process, the girls scared each other when one supposedly saw the shape of a coffin instead of a husband. In John Hale's book about the Salem Witch Trials only one girl, not a group of them, confessed to him afterward that she had tried this.

John Hale's account makes no mention of Tituba as having any part of the episode. He also does not identify when the incident took place.

The most infamous method used during the Salem Witch Trials was the touch test. Despite Parris warning his congregation against such examinations, the touch test was frequently used in Salem during this period.

In explanation the touch test was simple. If the accused touched the person that they had supposedly afflicted while the afflicted person was having a fit and the fit stopped, then the accused person was guilty.

One of the supposedly afflicted people later recounted, "we were blindfolded, and our hands were laid upon the afflicted persons, they being in their fits and falling into their fits at our coming into their presence, as they said. Some led us and laid our hands upon them, and then they said they were well and that we were guilty of afflicting them; whereupon we were all seized, as prisoners, by a warrant from the justice of the peace and forthwith carried to Salem."

Despite its frequency of use in Salem, as well as in other cases of alleged witchcraft the touch test was easily manipulated by the supposedly afflicted person.

Other dubious pieces of evidence were also employed to gain convictions during the Salem Witch Trials. These included the testimony by a confessed witch who identified others as witches. This was sometimes done by the accused in the hope that her compliance would lead to a leaner sentence.

Also taken into account was the discovery of poppits (poppets), books of palmistry and horoscopes, or pots of ointments in the possession or home of the accused. The observation of what were called witch's teats on the body of the accused was also taken as evidence even though they were easily faked.

A witch's teat was said to be a mole or blemish somewhere on the body that was insensitive to touch. The discovery of such insensitive areas was considered de facto evidence of witchcraft.

Much of this so-called evidence is little more than circumstantial and open to manipulation, often by those making the accusations.

How The Salem Witch Trials Are Concluded and Their Aftermath

With the conclusion of the Superior Court of Judicature, Court of Assize and General Goal Delivery in May 1693 the panic and hysteria that fueled the Salem Witch Trials was pretty much over.

Before the Salem Witch Trials had formerly ended accounts of the events were already being published. In 1692, Deodat Lawson, a former Salem Village minister, returned to the town.

After talking to many of those involved Lawson published an account of the event entitled 'A Brief and True Narrative of Some

Remarkable Passages Relating to Sundry Persons Afflicted by Witchcraft, at Salem Village: Which happened from the Nineteenth of March to the Fifth of April'.

This was followed by an account published in 1692 by "P.E. and J. A." (Philip English and John Alden) however the work is generally attributed to Samuel Willard, minister of the Third Church in Boston. The short piece is entitled 'Some Miscellany Observations On our present Debates respecting Witchcrafts, in a Dialogue Between S. & B.' S and B are Salem and Boston.

In the work S (Salem) and B (Boston) discuss the way the proceedings were being conducted. "B" urges caution about the use of testimony from the afflicted and the confessors, stating, "whatever comes from them is to be suspected, and it is dangerous using or crediting them too far".

The willingness to speak out against spectral evidence was, by now, only growing. Influential people such as Rev. William Milbourne, a Baptist minister in Boston, publicly petitioned the General Assembly in early June 1692.

This was followed by twelve local ministers submitting The Return of several Ministers to the Governor and Council in Boston that also cautioned the authorities against the use of spectral evidence.

In September 1692 at the request of the Governor of Massachusetts, Governor Phips, influential minister Cotton Mather wrote 'Wonders of the Invisible World: Being an Account of the Tryals of Several Witches,

Lately Executed in New-England'. Serving as a defense against the process the work was intended to "help very much flatten that fury which we now so much turn upon one another".

Published in both Boston and London 'Wonders of the Invisible World' opened with an introductory letter of endorsement by William Stoughton, the Chief Magistrate. The book included detailed accounts of five of the trials that had taken place.

Much of the information contained in the work Mather had copied directly from the court records, which were supplied to Mather by Stephen Sewall, his friend, and Clerk of the Court.

Following in his son's footsteps Increase Mather published 'Cases of Conscience

Concerning Evil Spirits' in the October of 1692. In it, Increase Mather again sternly cautioned against the reliance on spectral evidence, stating "It were better that Ten Suspected Witches should escape than that one Innocent Person should be Condemned".

The book was republished in both Boston and London in the following year. The third reprint also contained a 'Narrative' by Lawson and the anonymous "A Further Account of the Tryals of the New-England Witches, sent in a Letter from thence, to a Gentleman in London."

The production of these accounts marked a willingness to now openly speak out against the process of the witch trials. This willingness had started, albeit cautiously, while the trials were at their peak. After a few influential people had voiced their concern others felt more able to speak out. This sea change marked the start of public opinion turning against the Salem Witch Trials and ultimately signaled their end.

After the final trial had concluded in May 1693 the public response to the events continued. By now the tide had fully turned and survivors and family members of the accused along with other supporters began to campaign to clear the names of the accused.

The first indication that the public clamor for justice and the campaign to clear the names of those accused was not going to go away occurred in 1695. Thomas Maule, a prominent local Quaker, publicly criticised the trials held by the Puritans.

In his book 'Truth Held Forth and Maintained' Maule agreed with Increase Mather, writing "it was better that one hundred Witches should live than that one person be put to death for a witch, which is not a Witch". For publishing these views Thomas Maule was imprisoned for a year before a trial found him not guilty.

In response to this developing climate on the 17th of December 1696, the General Court ruled that the 14th of January 1697 would be a fast day. The day was to be used to reflect on the events of the previous few years.

On the 14th of January Reverend Samuel Willard, at the request of Samuel Sewall, read his apology to the congregation of Boston's South Church. The purpose of this was "to take the Blame & Shame" of the "late

Commission of Oyer & Terminer at Salem". This was followed by Thomas Fiske and eleven other trial jurors asking for forgiveness.

Between 1700 and 1703 numerous petitions were filed with the Massachusetts government, demanding that the convictions be formally reversed. Those tried and found guilty were considered dead in the eyes of the law, and with convictions still on the books, those not executed were vulnerable to further accusations.

The General Court initially reversed the attainder only for those who had been convicted but not executed: Abigail Faulkner Sr., Elizabeth Proctor, and Sarah Wardwell.

In 1703, another petition was filed, this time demanding a more equitable settlement for those wrongly accused. This was initially unsuccessful. It was not until 1709, when the General Court received a further request, that it took action on this proposal.

In May of that year twenty-two people who had been convicted of witchcraft, or whose relatives had been convicted of witchcraft, presented the government with a petition in which they demanded both a reversal of attainder and compensation for financial losses.

 Meanwhile in Salem Village church repentance for the witch trials was very much in evidence. Reverend Joseph Green and the members of the church voted on the 14th of February 1703, after almost two months of consideration, to reverse the excommunication of Martha Corey.

This was followed three years later on the 25th of August 1706 by Ann Putnam Jr, one of the most active accusers asking the congregation of Salem Village church for forgiveness.

She claimed that she had not acted out of malice, but had been deluded by Satan into denouncing innocent people, mentioning Rebecca Nurse in particular. Ann Putnam Jr's apology was accepted and she was subsequently granted full membership of the church.

On the 17th of October 1711, the General Court passed a bill reversing the judgment against the twenty-two people listed in the 1709 petition. The seven additional people who had been convicted but had not signed the petition received no such reversal of attainder.

Two months later, on the 17th of December Governor Joseph Dudley authorized monetary compensation to the twenty-two people in the 1709 petition. The amount of £578 12s was to be divided among the survivors and relatives of those accused. The majority of accounts were settled within a year. However, Phillip English's extensive claims were not settled until 1718.

Finally, on the 6th of March 1712, the reverend Nicholas Noyes and members of the Salem church reversed Noyes' earlier excommunications of Rebecca Nurse and Giles Corey.

Those who weren't exonerated in this initial period would now seemingly be forgotten for many years. In 1957, descendants of the six people who had been wrongly convicted and executed but who had not been included in the bill for a reversal of attainder in 1711, or added to it in 1712, demanded that the General Court formally clear their ancestor's names.

While this resulted in the passing of an Act only Ann Pudeator was named, the others were listed as "certain other persons". A strange phrasing, which meant that Bridget Bishop, Susannah Martin, Alice Parker, Wilmot Redd and Margaret Scott, were never formally cleared by name.

With the sense of justice, this provided the community of Salem felt an ease in the tensions which had haunted their village over the previous few years. The families of the victims now turned their attention to commemorating their relatives.

As the dust settled on the Salem itch Trials people began to speculate the underlying cause for the events. One suggestion is that the main driving force behind the hysteria was a feud between two prominent Salem families.

The first three people accused and arrested for allegedly afflicting Betty Parris, Abigail Williams, Ann Putnam Jr and Elizabeth Hubbard were Sarah Good. Sarah Osborne and Tituba. Today some historians believe that the accusation made by Ann Putnam Jr. Was motivated by a family feud. This family feud fuelled many of the accusations, which occurred during the witch trials.

In the years preceding the Salem Witch Trials a vicious rivalry had erupted between the Putnam and Porter families. This subsequently polarised the people of Salem. Citizens would often have heated debates, which escalated into full-fledged fighting, based solely on their opinion of the feud.

Originally from Buckinghamshire, England, the Putnam family led by John and Priscilla Putnam moved to Salem, Massachusetts in around 1634. John and Priscilla brought their children with them including three sons; Thomas, Nathaniel, and John.

The head of the family, John Putnam, was a dutiful and successful settler. He was granted a piece of land as were each of his sons. These three boys would eventually all have children of their own. It was this third generation of Putnam settlers, in particular, the children of the eldest son Thomas, who were involved in Salem's witch trial frenzy.

When the colonists arrived at the Massachusetts Bay Colony and settled Salem they soon found that the land in the immediate vicinity was not fertile. This discovery saw many of the settlers moving to smaller, farming communities outside the original city limits.

One such community was Salem Farms located around five miles north of Salem. The Putnam family controlled much of the land in the Salem Farms area.

Originally these outer lands, which surrounded Salem Town, did not have separate identities, this meant that the farmers were required to be members of the

Church of Salem. However, over time, as settlements began to grow outside the larger community of Salem, some began to break away and form independent towns.

The first of these was Wenham, which was established in 1643. Desiring autonomy from the larger city as well as their own church, Salem Village began to petition for their independence in the late 1660's.

The officials of Salem Town refused their request. This refusal would drive a wedge between the two communities as many members of Salem Village began to resent the power that Salem Town held over them.

As well as driving a wedge between the town of Salem and Salem Village this debate also divided Salem village. Some of the farmers and villagers wished to remain part of Salem Town while others were keen to have their independence.

Eventually, in 1672, Salem Village was granted the right to build their own church and hire a minister. However, the villagers would officially remain members of the Salem Town Church, which would govern the smaller parish.

The village was also permitted to establish a committee of five, to assess and gather taxes from the villagers - including church-members and non-church members, for the ministry.

For the first time, Salem Village had a degree of autonomy. While this should have resolved the tensions now present in Salem Village, in reality, the right to build their own church only made the situation in Salem worse.

Of the two warring factions, two families emerged as leaders of the separate factions -- the Putnams and the Porters. In many ways they were similar; both families were early settlers of the Massachusetts Bay Colony, both families had been successful, and both were large landowners in Salem Village.

The Putnams were farmers who followed the simple and austere lifestyle of traditional Puritans. They, along with other farmers in Salem Village, believed that the thriving economy of Salem Town, and more specifically, thriving merchants, made people too individualistic. This stood in stark contrast to the communal nature that Puritanism mandated.

On the opposite side the Porters derived much of their wealth from agricultural operations, they were also entrepreneurs who developed commercial interests in Salem Town as well as other areas and were active in the governmental affairs of the larger community.

Due to these differing viewpoints, the Porters' diversified business interests allowed them to increase their family's wealth, becoming one of the wealthiest families in the area. In the meantime, the Putnam family wealth was stagnating.

The Putnams, like other farming families, had campaigned for independence from Salem Town; while the Porters preferred the link between the two Salems to remain.

Adding fuel to the flames, in 1672, a Porter owned dam and sawmill was responsible for flooding much of the Putnam farmland. This led to the Putnam family taking out a lawsuit against the Porters.

Having gained the right to build their own church and gain their own minister, the Putnams also sought to "control" the church, thereby, controlling the community. Heading up this group was Thomas Putnam Jr., who forged an elite group that would remain in control of the village affairs for years.

His allies included his brother, Edward Putnam, brother-in-law, Jonathan Walcott; Walcott's uncle, the innkeeper Nathaniel Ingersoll, and other Salem Church deacons, committeemen, and church elders.

By the time Reverend Samuel Parris arrived in Salem the separation between the town and village churches was increasing. On the 19th of November 1689, the Salem Village church charter was finally signed and Reverend Samuel Parris became Salem Village's first ordained minister.

Salem Village was now separate from Salem Town. This only intensified the Putnam Porter family conflict.

With the village still divided on the 16th of October 1691, the Porter faction took control of the village committee from the Putnam's.

Some of those now on the committee included Daniel Andrew, John Porter Sr's son in law, Joseph Hutchinson who was responsible for operating the sawmills that had flooded the Putnams' farms, Francis

Nurse a village farmer who had been involved in a bitter boundary dispute with Nathaniel Putnam and Joseph Porter the half-brother of Thomas Porter Jr.

The new committee quickly voted down a tax levy that would have raised revenue to pay the salary of Reverend Parris. This infuriated the Putnam faction.

Embittered, the minister avenged this refusal by proclaiming in his sermons that a conspiracy against the church had been hatched within the village. He even went so far as to assert that the Devil had taken possession of some of the villagers.

In addition to the Porters, Thomas Putman, Jr. also had a lengthy list of other perceived enemies, including the Howe, Towne, Hobbs and Wildes families of Topsfield, with whom he had engaged in land disputes with. Another was John Proctor, who had gained a license for a tavern with the stipulation that he could not sell liquor to locals.

This made Proctor's tavern a rendezvous point for "outsiders." The business was also in direct competition with Thomas Putman Jr's ally, Nathaniel Ingersoll. Other enemies included Daniel Andrews and Philip English who were closely associated the Porter family.

It was against this background that the witch hysteria began in early 1692.

The first to be afflicted were the reverend Samuel Parris' daughter Elizabeth and his niece Abigail Williams who lived in the parsonage with Parris and his family. Soon, other young members of the community also began to have fits including Thomas Putman's daughter Ann Putnam Jr, his niece Mary Walcott, and a servant girl who lived in the Putnam household named Mercy Lewis.

As the sufferers of witchcraft were believed to be the victims of a crime, the community set out to find the perpetrators.

On February 29, 1692, under intense adult questioning, Elizabeth Parris and Abigail Williams named Sarah Good, Sarah Osborne, and Tituba as their tormentors. These five "afflicted girls" would become the most fervent of the accusers. The majority of those they accused were enemies of the Putnams.

If you believe that the Salem Witch Trials were borne out of more than just a desire by the Putnam family to gain revenge on their enemies there are other possible explanations for what happened in the puritanical stronghold of Salem.

Today it is not accepted that the symptoms exhibited by the supposedly possessed during the Salem witch trials and in other witch hunts is caused by bewitchment. A number of other medical based suggestions have been put forward.

One such explanation is ergot poisoning.

A widely known theory about the cause of the reported afflictions holds that the ingestion of bread, which has been made from rye grain that has been infected by a fungus, Claviceps purpurea, is the cause of the symptoms.

This fungus is commonly known as ergot. It contains chemicals similar to those used in the synthetic psychedelic drug LSD. Convulsive ergotism can cause a variety of symptoms, including nervous dysfunction.

The theory that ergot poisoning was the cause of symptoms exhibited by the girls in Salem was first widely publicised in 1976 when graduate student Linnda R. Caporael published an article in Science journal. In her article, she theorized that the hallucinations of the afflicted girls were the result of ingesting rye bread that had been made with moldy grain.

Within a few months, a second article disagreeing with this theory was published in the same journal. Authored by Spanos and Gottlieb the article was based on a wider assessment of the historical records, examining all the symptoms reported by those claiming affliction.

Spanos and Gottlieb concluded that ergot poisoning has additional symptoms that were not reported by those claiming affliction in Salem. Also if the poison were in the villages food supply, a wider range of people and not just certain individuals would have reported symptoms.

This second article also argued that biological symptoms do not start and end based on external cues, which is what supposedly happened in Salem. Nor do biological symptoms start and stop simultaneously across a group of people, again this supposedly occurred in the Salem case.

In 1999, Laurie Winn Carlson offered an alternative medical theory, that those afflicted in Salem suffered from encephalitis lethargica. This is a disease whose symptoms match some of what was reported in Salem and could have been spread by birds and other animals.

M. M. Drymon proffered a third theory; Lyme disease was responsible for witches and witch affliction. Drymon found that many of the afflicted in Salem and elsewhere lived in areas that had a high risk of ticks. Many of the afflicted had a variety of red marks and rashes that looked like bite marks on their skin, and suffered from neurological and arthritic symptoms.

In 2012 an outbreak in Le Roy, New York saw some girls suffering from "Salem-like" symptoms. Some of these girls tested positive for Lyme disease.

An altogether different theory comes from the fact that concurrent with the Salem Witch Trials was King Phillip's War. It has been suggested that Post-Traumatic Stress Disorder was present in some of the accusers.

The Wabanaki, allies of the French, attacked British colonists in Maine, New Hampshire, and northern Massachusetts in a series of guerrilla skirmishes. The survivors of these attacks blamed colonial leaders for the success of the attacks, accusing them of incompetence, cowardice, and corruption.

With the success of these attacks a climate of fear and panic pervaded the northern coastline. This prompted a flood of refugees to head for southern Massachusetts and beyond. Some of those who fled the attacks found a new life as maidservants in Salem, they were also accusers in the witch trials.

Witnessing a violent attack, such as the raids by the Wabanaki, is a trigger for hysteria and posttraumatic stress disorder.

Not only might the violence of the border skirmishes to the north explain symptoms of P.T.S.D. in accusers who formerly lived among the slaughtered, but also the widespread blame of elite incompetence for those attacks offers an explanation for the unusual demographic among the accused. Traditionally witch trial 'defendants' had been overwhelmingly female, and members of the lower classes.

In the Salem Witch Trials, this pattern was broken. Many elite men were accused of witchcraft; some of them were the same leaders who failed to successfully protect besieged settlements to the north. This anomaly in the pattern of typical witch trials, combined with widespread blame for the northern attacks on colonial leadership, suggests the relevance of the northern guerrilla attacks to the accusers.

In a similar vein, others have suggested that hysteria and other psychosomatic disorders caused much of what was seen in Salem.

Indeed the symptoms displayed by the afflicted in Salem are similar to those seen in classic cases of hysteria.

This is the view of Marion Starkey and Chadwick Hansen. Physicians have latterly replaced the vague diagnosis of hysteria with what is essentially its synonym, psychosomatic disorder.

Psychological processes known to influence physical health are now called "psychosomatic". They include: "several types of the disease known as somatoform disorders, in which somatic symptoms appear either without any organic disorder or without organic damage that can account for the severity of the symptoms".

A second type, conversion disorders, involves "organically inexplicable malfunctions in motor and sensory systems". The third type, pain disorder, involves "sensation either in the absence of an organic problem or in excess of actual physical damage."

Psychologists Nicholas P. Spanos and Jack Gottlieb believe that the afflicted in Salem were enacting the roles that maintained their definition of themselves as bewitched.

This in return allowed the belief to grow in many of the accused that the symptoms, such as bites, pinches, and pricks, were produced by specters. These symptoms were typically apparent throughout the community and caused an internal disease process.

Others have acknowledged that, while the afflicted girls were physically healthy before their fits began, they were not spiritually well because they of the pressures which came from living in an adult world that did not cater to their needs as children.

The basis for a Puritan society, which entails the possibility for sin, damnation, common internal quarrels and the strict outlook on marriage, repressed the unmarried teenagers who felt damnation was imminent.

It is theorized that the young girls longed for the freedom to move beyond their low status in society. As an escape, the girls indulged in the forbidden conduct of fortune telling with the Indian slave Tituba to discover whom their future husbands were.

This eventually resulted in them suffering from hysteria as they tried to cope with "the consequences of a conflict between conscience (or at least fear of discovery) and the unhallowed craving."

Their symptoms of excessive weeping, silent states followed by violent screams, hiding under furniture, and hallucinations can all be symptoms of hysteria.

Marion Starkey points out that after the crisis at Salem had calmed it was discovered that diagnosed insanity appeared in the Parris family. Likewise, the Putnam family had a history of illness.

Ann Putnam Jr.'s mother experienced paranoid tendencies from previous tragedies in her life. When Ann Jr. began to experience hysterical fits, her symptoms verged on psychotic. Marion Starkey argues that this was a case of hysteria. As the suffering girls began to receive more attention they used it as a means to rebel against the restrictions of Puritanism.

A differing point of view, Hansen approaches the afflicted girls through a pathological lens. Hansen argues that the girls suffered from clinical hysteria because of the fear of witchcraft, not witchcraft itself.

The girls feared bewitchment and experienced symptoms that were all in the girls' heads. Hansen contests that "if you believe in witchcraft and you discover that someone has been melting your wax image over a slow fire ... the probability is that you will get extremely sick – your symptoms will be psychosomatic rather than organic."

The girls suffered from what appeared to be bite marks and would often try to throw themselves into fires. Both of these are classic symptoms of hysteria. Hansen explains that hysterics will often try to injure themselves, which never result in serious injuries because they wait until someone is present to stop them.

Hansen also concludes that skin lesions are the most common psychosomatic symptom among hysterics, which can resemble bite or pinch marks on the skin. Hansen believes the girls are not accountable for their actions because they were not consciously responsible in committing them.

A final theory emerged in the 1970s. Proposed by historian John Demos the suggestion that the afflicted girls were "projecting" soon gained support. Demos adopted a psycho-historical approach to look at the unusual behavior suffered by the afflicted girls in Salem.

Demos combined the disciplines of anthropology and psychology to propose that psychological projection could explain the violent fits the girls were experiencing. Demos observed that most of the accused were predominantly married or widowed women between the ages of forty-one and sixty, while the afflicted girls were primarily adolescent girls.

The structure of the Puritan community created internal conflict among the young girls who felt controlled by the older women leading to internal feelings of resentment.

Demos asserts that often neighborly relations within the Puritan community remained tense and most witchcraft episodes began after some sort of conflict or encounter between neighbors. The accusation of witchcraft was a means of displaying any suppressed anger and resentment felt. The violent fits and verbal attacks experienced at Salem were directly related to the process of projection.

Demos asserts that the violent fits displayed, often aimed at figures of authority, were attributed to bewitchment because it allowed the afflicted youth to project their repressed aggression and not be directly held responsible for their behavior because they were coerced by the Devil.

Therefore, aggression experienced because of witchcraft became an outlet and the violent fits and the physical attacks endured, inside and outside the courtroom, were examples of how each girl was undergoing the psychological process of projection.

Whatever the underlying cause the residents of Salem and the families of those accused have long since turned their attention to commemorating those who wrongly lost their lives.

The descendants of Rebecca Nurse erected an obelisk-shaped granite memorial in her memory in 1885 on the grounds of the Nurse family homestead. This was joined in 1892 by a second monument in honor of the forty neighbors who had stood in support of Rebecca Nurse.

A series of events were held in Salem and the surrounding area in 1992 to commemorate three hundred years since the witch trials. One of these was the dedication of a memorial park in Salem.

The park included stone slab benches inserted in the wall of the park for each of those executed in 1692. Speakers at the ceremony included playwright Arthur Miller and Nobel Laureate Elie Wiesel. Salem Village, now known as Danvers, erected its own new memorial and also held a ceremony to re-inter bones unearthed in the 1950s which are assumed to be those of George Jacobs, Sr.

In 1992, The Danvers Tercentennial Committee also persuaded the Massachusetts House of Representatives to issue a resolution honoring those who had died.

After extensive efforts by Paula Keene, a Salem schoolteacher, state representatives J. Michael Ruane and Paul Tirone and others a bill was issued. This saw the names of all those not previously listed added to the resolution.

When the resolution was finally signed on October 31, 2001, by Governor Jane Swift all those accused were, 300 years after the first event, now declared innocent.

The University of Virginia, after months of work, in January 2016, announced that its project team had determined the execution site on Gallows Hill in Salem.

At this site nineteen "witches" had been hanged in public. Members of the Gallows Hill Project had worked with the city of Salem using old maps and documentation, as well as sophisticated GIS and ground-penetrating radar technology, to survey the area that had became known as Proctor's Ledge. There are now plans for a memorial to be constructed on the site to honor the innocent victims of the Salem Witch Trials.

Today the Salem Witch Trials are well known throughout the western world. The events which took place in 17th century Salem have captured the imagination of writers and artists countless times in the years that have followed.

Many of these interpretations have taken liberties with the facts of the historical episode in the name of artistic license. However accurate the retelling the legend of what happened in the puritan stronghold of Salem has only proceeded to grow.

Printed in Great Britain
by Amazon